Cold December Winds

A New Collection of Old Christmas Carols
Arranged for Lap Harp

by
Suzanne Guldimann
Illustrated by the author

WEST OF THE MOON BOOKS
Malibu, California

For Thomas and Elizabeth,
with love.

And so, at this Christmas time, I greet you.
Not quite as the world sends greetings,
but with profound esteem, and with the prayer that
for you, now and forever, the day breaks,
and the shadows flee away.

—Fra Giovanni, 1513

My thanks and deepest gratitude to my parents,
and to Anna, Carolee, Margaret, and Sylvia,
for all of their help.

Published by West of the Moon Books
P.O. Box 6133, Malibu, California 90264

Cold December Winds
Copyright © 2001 Suzanne Guldimann
Illustrations copyright © 2001 Suzanne Guldimann
Revised Third Edition © 2023

ISBN 979-8-9886065-0-5

Table of Contents

About the Pieces

All of the pieces in this book can be played on a lap harp with a range of just two and a half octaves (from C up to G). Although, on a small harp you will need to play an octave higher than the music is written, treating middle C as low C. The pieces can also be played on a larger harp, or on guitar, violin, flute, recorder, or any melody instrument. On a larger harp you may wish to add some additional chords. To keep the pieces easy to play on small harps with limited sharping levers, I've arranged them in the keys of C and G, and their minors and modes.

The carols in this collection are drawn from many countries, and span many centuries of history. Many are from the medieval and Renaissance periods, but others are folk carols that belong to later periods, or whose origins are uncertain. Many of the pieces in this collection are well known and much loved, and some are unusual, and rarely heard. I have attempted to keep the historical and regional flavor and character of each piece, and whenever possible, I have included lyrics in the original language, together with a version in English.

Introduction

When I finished writing my first book of carols, Green Grows the Holly, I was dismayed at the number of beautiful and wonderful things I did not have room for. Four years and three books later, I had the chance to return to carols, and put together a second collection. The first book was strictly medieval and Renaissance. This volume has many carols from those periods as well, but it also has folk carols from throughout Europe. There are even a couple from the United States. Although separated in time and distance they have in common the joy and beauty of the celebration of Christmas.

Most of the oldest surviving carols are preserved in handwritten manuscripts. Many of these carols had fallen out of use, only to be rediscovered in the nineteenth and twentieth centuries. A few rare pieces have endured for centuries. The "Te Deum Laudamus" is one of these. Although its original music is lost, its text has been sung at Christmas, and on New Year's Day, for nearly fifteen hundred years. Theodoricus Petri's great sixteenth century collection of songs, Piae Cantiones, preserves a wealth of early carols. The manuscript, dated 1582, contains songs from many parts of Europe, some dating back as far as the thirteenth century.

In Great Britain, broadsides preserved many traditional Christmas carols. These inexpensive printed black letter sheets, sold for pennies, were popular from the sixteenth century through the nineteenth century. However, they more often then not contained only the lyrics; everyone was expected to know the music. Britain also has a large number of instrumental music manuscripts, many dating to the Elizabethan period. Some of these provide the missing music to accompany the broadside lyrics.

Most of the later carols come from the folk tradition. Because of the lack of written documentation, these are difficult to accurately date. Many were collected in the nineteenth century, when there was already the growing awareness that the traditions throughout Europe were beginning to slip away. Early collectors ranged from Davies Gilbert and William Sandys, who collected many of what are today the best known and loved English carols, to Carl Riedel, and Charles Bordes, who gathered songs in Bohemia, and the Basque mountains, respectively.

In France, many of the most beautiful noëls were rescued from oblivion by the composers of the seventeenth and eighteenth century. Jean François Dandrieu, Louis-Claude Daquin, and Claude-Bénigne Balbastre, preserved and popularized many of the early French carols in their arrangements for organ. Other noëls have remained enduringly popular, still sung in churches and homes at Christmas time. The German speaking countries have also preserved many of their earliest carols as church music, and popular carols, that have been sung in an unbroken tradition since the fifteenth century. Italy and Spain have many carols with roots in medieval traditions, as well. Spain, in particular, has a long history of beautiful carols, many dating to the sixteenth century.

In America, a unique collection of hymns gathered by William Walker in the early eighteenth century provides the oldest record of many early American carols. Walker composed a number of the pieces himself, but the majority were collected from the oral tradition. He called his collection a "shape note" hymnal, because each note had a different shape, to make them easier to recognize and sing for people who could not read music. Walker's Southern Harmony was tremendously popular, and has remained almost constantly in print since its publication in 1835. It was the first of many shape note collections.

I took the title of this book from an old Catalán carol. Its anonymous lyrics hold the essence of the Christmas spirit. In the dark of winter they turn towards the hope of spring, and the promise of redemption.

Cold December's winds were stilled
In the month of snowing.
As the world in darkness slept,
Springtime's hope was growing.

—Anonymous

A Solis Ortus Cardine
From Lands that See the Sun Arise

A beautiful and ancient Christmas hymn written by the fifth century poet Caelius Sedulius, "A Solis Ortus Cardine" was traditionally sung at lauds (morning service) on Christmas day. A number of versions have survived, the earliest dating to the twelfth century. The setting given here is from the seventeenth century, and is attributed to the German composer, Heinrich Schütz. The English translation is from the nineteenth century, and was written by J.M. Neale (1818-1866), and J. Ellerton (1826-1893).

Sharp the G above middle C, and
watch for lever change in measue 8.

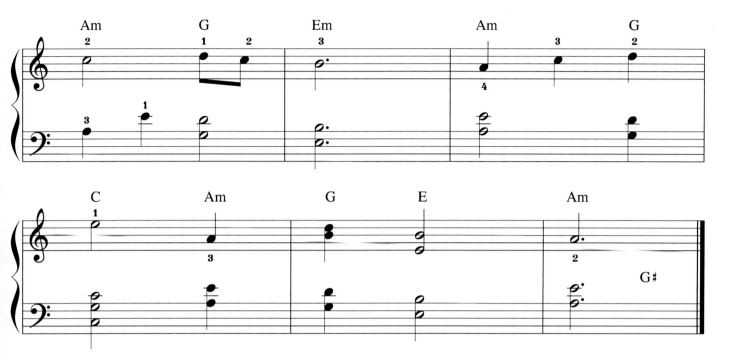

A solis ortus cardine	From lands that see the sun arise,
Et usque terrae limitem	To earth's remotest boundaries,
Christum canamus Principem,	The virgin born today we sing,
Natum Maria Virgine.	The Son of Mary, Christ the King.
Beatus Auctor seculi	Behold, the world's Creator wears
Servile corpus induit,	The form and fashion of a slave;
Ut, carne carnem liberans	Our very flesh our Maker shares,
Non perderet quos condidit.	His fallen creature, man, to save.
Feno iacere pertulit,	He shrank not from the oxen's stall,
Praesepe non abhorruit,	He lay within the manger bed,
Parvoque lacte pastus est	And He whose bounty feedeth all,
Per quem nec ales esurit.	At Mary's breast himself was fed.
Gaudet chorus celestium	And while the angels in the sky
Et Angeli canunt Deum,	Sang praise above the silent field,
Palamque fit pastoribus	To shepherds poor the Lord most high,
Pastor, Creator omnium.	The one great Shepherd was revealed.
Gloria tibi, Domine,	Eternal praise, and glory be,
Qui natus es de Virgine,	O Jesu, virgin born, to thee;
Cum Patre et Sancto Spiritu,	With Father and with Holy Ghost,
In sempiterna secula.	From men and from the heavenly host.

Apple Tree Wassail

A wassail song from Somerset, in the south of England. Wassailing traditionally took place between Christmas and Epiphany. Some wassailing songs were sung from door to door to bring luck, others were performed in the orchards, for the benefit of the apple trees. The ancient custom is believed to get its name from the Anglo-Saxon greeting, "wes hál," or "be well."

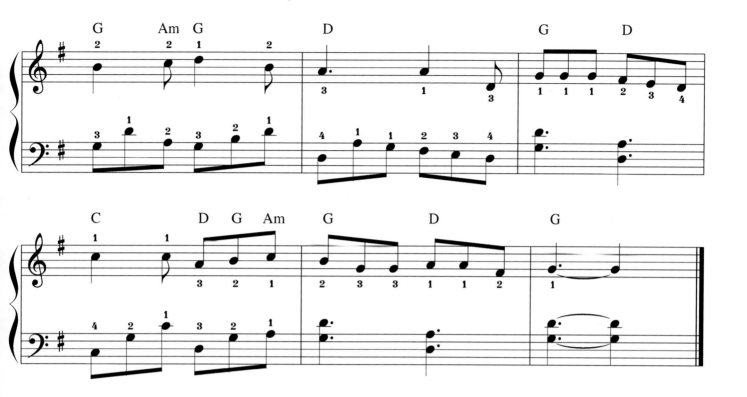

Old apple tree, we'll wassail thee,
And hoping thou wilt bear.
The Lord doth know where we shall be,
To be merry another year.
To blow well, and to bear well,
And so merry let us be.
Let every man drink up his cup,
And health to the old apple tree!

Shouted at the conclusion:

Apples now, hats full, caps full,
Three bushel bags full,
Barrels full, barn's floors full,
And a little heap under the stairs!
Hip hip hooroo! Hip hip hooroo!
Hip hip hooroo!

The Babe of Bethlehem

An early American folk carol with many variants. William Walker collected this version from the oral tradition, and it became one of the best known and loved pieces in his shape-note hymnal, Southern Harmony, first published in 1835. The melody has been used for many songs, both spiritual and secular. It may have originally come from Ireland.

10

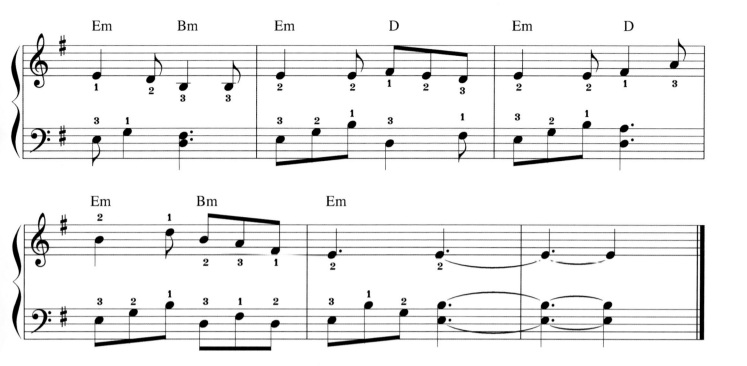

Ye nations all, on you I call, come hear this declaration,
And don't refuse this glorious news of Jesus and salvation.
To royal Jews came first the news of Christ, the great Messiah,
As was foretold by prophets old, Isaiah, Jeremiah.

His parents poor in earthly store, to entertain the stranger,
They found no bed to lay his head, but in the ox's manger:
No royal things, as used by kings, were seen by those that found him,
But in the hay the stranger lay, with swaddling bands around him.

On that same night a glorious light to shepherds there appeared,
Bright angels came in shining flame, they saw and greatly feared.
The angels said: "Be not afraid, although we much alarm you,
We do appear, good news to bear, as now we will inform you."

"The city's name is Bethlehem, in which God has appointed,
This glorious morn a Saviour's born, for him God has anointed;
By this you'll know, if you will go, to see this little stranger,
His lovely charms in Mary's arms, both lying in a manger."

When this was said, straightway was made a glorious sound from heaven;
Each flaming tongue an anthem sung: "To men a Saviour's given;
In Jesus' name, the glorious theme, we elevate our voices;
At Jesus' birth be peace on earth, meanwhile all heaven rejoices."

Then with delight they took their flight, and wing'd their way to glory;
The shepherds gazed, and were amazed, to hear the pleasing story.
To Bethlehem they quickly came, the glorious news to carry,
And in the stall they found them all, Joseph, the Babe, and Mary.

Basque Carol
The Angel Gabriel

This is one of the best known and most beautiful of the traditional Basque carols. The text is medieval, although the tune dates to the eighteenth century. The Basque name for the carol is "Birjina gaztettobat zegoen." The English lyrics are a paraphrase of the original Basque, and were written by the famous British antiquarian, Sabine Baring-Gould (1834-1924), who is better known as the author of the text to the hymn, "Onward Christian Soldiers."

Sharp the G above middle C.

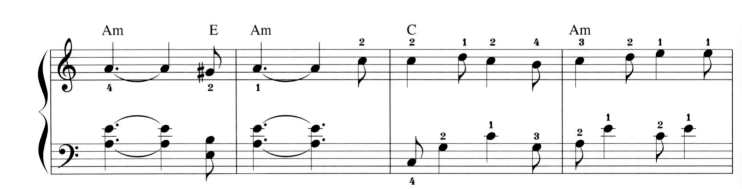

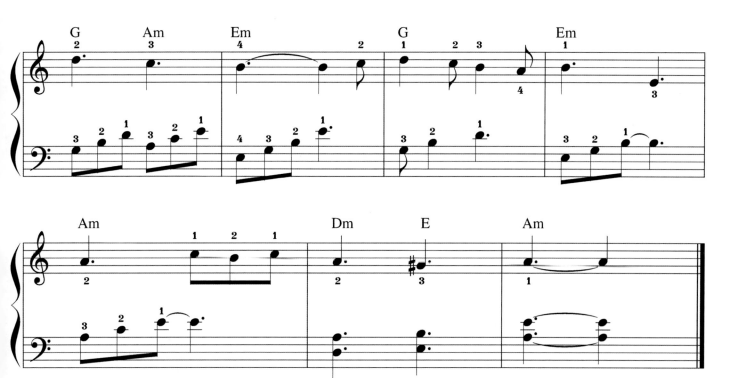

The angel Gabriel from Heaven came,
His wings as drifted snow,
His eyes as flame; "All hail," said he,
"Thou lowly maiden Mary."
Most highly favoured lady, Gloria!

"For known a blessed Mother thou shalt be,
All generations laud and honour thee:
Thy Son shall be Emmanuel, by seers foretold."
Most highly favoured lady, Gloria!

Then gentle Mary meekly bowed her head,
"To me be as it pleaseth God," she said,
"My soul shall laud and magnify his holy name."
Most highly favoured lady, Gloria!

Of her Emmanuel, the Christ, was born
In Bethlehem, all on a Christmas morn,
And Christian folk throughout the world will ever say:
Most highly favoured lady, Gloria!

Canzone di Zampoguari
Carol of the Bagpipers

It was an ancient tradition in southern Italy for the shepherds to come into the cities during the last week of Advent, to play their pipes at shrines and churches. This is a seventeenth century shepherds' carol from Naples. The zampogna is a large bagpipe with two drones and two chanters. Handel used the melody of this carol in The Messiah, *for the aria, "He Shall Feed His Flock."*

14

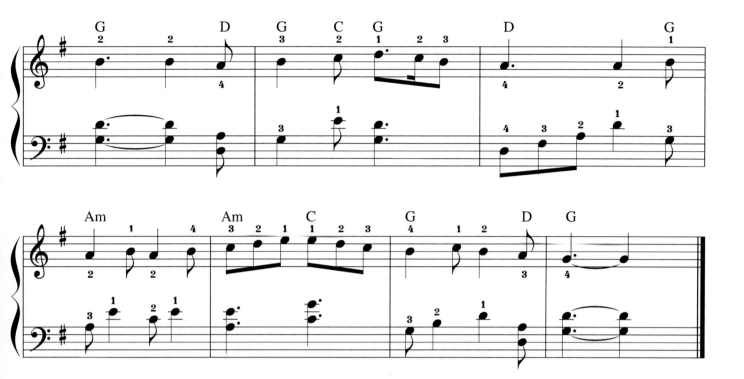

Quando nascette Ninno
A Betlemme,
Era notte e pareva miezojuorno!
Maje le stelle
Lustre e belle,
Se vedèttero accusí!
E'a cchiù lucente
Jette a chiammà
Li Magi, n Oriente.

Non c'erano nemice
Pe' la terra,
La pecora pasceva co' lo lione,
Co le crapette
Se vedette
Lo liopardo pazzeá:
L'urzo e' o vitiello,
E co' lo lupo 'mpace
O' pecoriello.

When Christ the Lord was born
At Bethlehem afar,
Although twas night,
There shone as bright as day a brilliant star.
Never so brightly, never so whitely,
Shone the stars as on that night
A glorious message they sent
To light the way and guide the Magi
From the Orient.

The lion and the lamb,
When Christ was born on earth,
In peace lay down beside each other,
Rejoicing at His birth.
Cattle and leopards, wolves, sheep and shepherds,
Gather together without any fear,
Now that our Saviour is here.
And in the skies the angel proclaims;
On earth a paradise.

The Cherry Tree Carol
Joseph Was an Old Man

A tremendously popular carol, with enough versions to fill an entire book of its own. "The Cherry Tree Carol" is really a ballad, and not a carol at all. It has its origins in the fifteenth century, and may once have been part of the Coventry mystery plays. The legend that forms the basis of the ballad dates to the fifth century. Originally, the tree was not a cherry tree, but a date palm. The ballad has a bewildering array of verses and melodies. This version can be found in both Great Britain, and across the Atlantic, in the Appalachian Mountains.

Do not sharp the F above middle C.

16

Joseph was an old man, and an old man was he,
When he wedded Mary in the land of Galilee.

Joseph and Mary walked through an orchard good,
Where was cherries and berries as red as any blood.

O then bespoke Mary, so meek and so mild,
"Pluck me a cherry, Joseph, for I am with child."

O then spoke Joseph, with words most unkind,
"Let him pluck thee a cherry that got thee with child."

O then bespoke the Babe within His mother's womb,
"Bow down then the tallest tree for my mother to have some."

Then bowed down the highest tree unto His mother's hand:
Then she cried: "See, Joseph, I have cherries at my command!"

O then bespoke Joseph: "I have done Mary wrong.
But cheer up, my dearest, and be not cast down."

Then Mary plucked a cherry as red as any blood;
And Mary went home again with her heavy load.

Cold December's Winds

El Decembre Congelat

An ancient and very beautiful folk carol from the Catalán region of Spain, which has become popular in both the United States and Britain. The image of the rose blooming in the snow appears many times in medieval Christmas legends. This is a true "carol," in that it was originally intended to be danced, as well as sung.

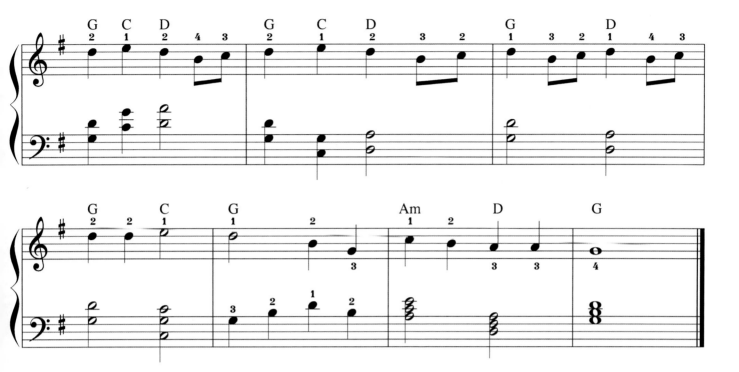

El desembre congelat,
Confús es retira.
Abril de flors coronat,
Tot el món admira,
Quan en un jardi d'amor
Neix una divina flor.
D'una ro, ro, ro,
D'una sa, sa, sa,
D'una ro, d'una sa,
D'una rosa bella,
Fecunda y poncella.

El primer Pare causá
Le nit tenevrosa
Que a tot el mon ofusca
La vista penosa
Mes en una mitjà nit
Brilla el sol que n'és eixit
D'una bel, bel, bel,
D'una la, la, la,
D'una bel, d'una la,
D'una bella aurora
Que el cel enamora.

Cold December's winds were stilled
In the month of snowing.
As the world in darkness slept,
Springtime's Hope was growing;
Then one rose-tree blossomed new,
One sweet Flower on it grew.
On the tree once bare,
Grew the Rose so fair,
Ah, the Rose, ah, the Rose,
Ah the Rose tree blooming,
Sweet the air perfuming.

When the darkness fell that night,
Bringing sweet reposing,
All the land was hid from sight,
Sleep our eyes now closing.
Suddenly, there came a gleam
From the sky, the wondrous beam
Of a heav'nly star,
Giving light afar;
Ah, the star, ah, the star,
Ah, the star-beam glowing,
Brightness ever growing.

In Those Twelve Days

A New Dial

Twelve days of Christmas, twelve hours in the day, twelve divisions on the face of a clock or sun dial (hence the name, "A New Dial"). The earliest version of this carol appears in an almanac published in 1625. It is however, most likely much older, several of the verses hint at early medieval origins. This version is from the Cornish folk tradition, and dates to the eighteenth century. It appears in the collections of both Davies Gilbert and William Sandys. There is an echo of this ancient carol in the American spiritual, "My Children Go Where I Send Thee."

Sharp the G above middle C.

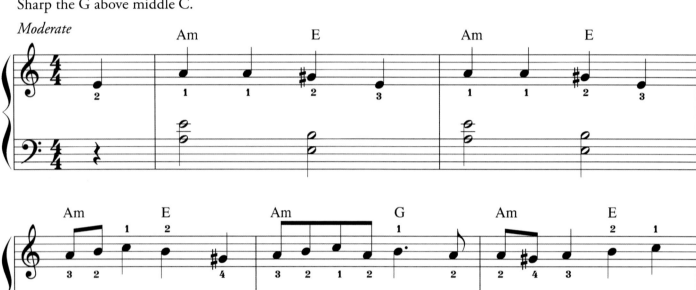

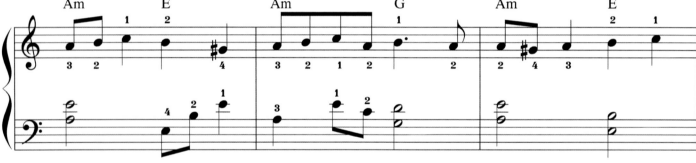

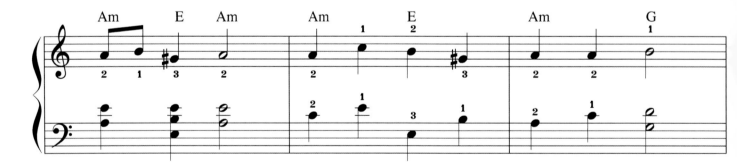

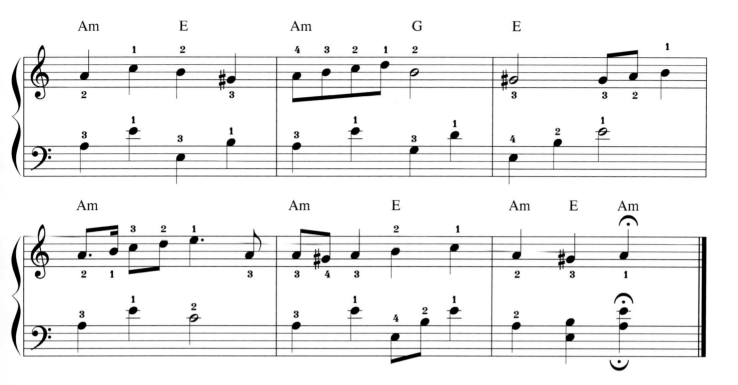

In those twelve days let us be glad,
In those twelve days let us be glad,
For God of his power
Hath all things made.

What is that which is but one?
What is that which is but one?
We have but one God alone
In Heaven above sits on his throne.

In those twelve days etc.

What are they that are but two?
What are they that are etc.
Two testaments, as we are told,
The one is New and the other Old.

Three persons in the Trinity,
The Father, the Son, and the Ghost Holy.

Four gospels written true,
John, Luke, Mark and Mathew.

Five senses we have to tell,
God grant us grace to use them well.

Six ages this world shall last,
Five of them are gone and past.

Seven days in the week have we,
Six to work and one holy.

Eight beatitudes are given,
Use them well and go to Heaven.

Nine degrees of angels high
Which praise God continually.

Ten commandments God hath given,
Keep them right and go to Heaven.

Eleven with Christ above do dwell,
The Twelfth forever burns in Hell.

Twelve days are there in Christmastide
Rejoice, and in good faith abide.

Count one the first hour of thy Birth,
The hours that follow, lead to Earth;
Count Twelve thy doleful striking knell,
And then thy Dial shall go well.

Kommet ihr Hirten
Come, Shepherds

A Bohemian carol that has become popular in German speaking countries. The text may once have belonged to a shepherd play. The carol was collected and popularized in the 1870s by the composer, Carl Riedel. The tune is also traditionally used for the Czech carol, "Nesem Vam Noviny." I was unable to find a suitable English version of the text, so I have included a literal translation, instead.

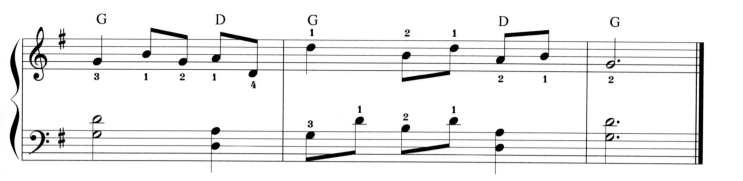

Kommet, ihr Hirten, Ihr Männer und Frau'n!
Kommet, das liebliche Kindlein zu schaun!
Christus, der Herr, ist heute geboren,
Den Gott zum Heiland euch hat erkoren.
Fürchtet euch nicht!

Lasset uns sehen in Bethlehems Stall,
Was uns verheißten der himmlische Schall!
Was wir dort finden, lasset uns künden,
Lasset uns preisen in frommen Weisen.
Allelujah!

Wahrlich, die Engel verkündigen heut'
Bethlehems Hirtenvolk gar große Freud':
Nun soll es werden Frieden auf Erden,
Den Menschen allen ein Wohlgefallen.
Ehre sei Gott!

Come all ye shepherds, Come men and women,
Come lovely child with hair like flax.
Christ the Lord is born today,
He whom God in heaven has sent to us.
Be not afraid!

Come, now let us see, in Bethlehem's stable,
What was promised us by the heavenly song.
What shall we find there, let us announce,
Let us praise in pious ways.
Allelujah!

Truly the angel proclaims aloud this day
To Bethlehem's shepherds, a wonderous joy:
Now there shall be Peace on Earth,
For all mankind a blessing.
Praise be to God!

Let All that Are to Mirth Inclined

A popular English broadside carol which dates to the middle of the seventeenth century, and may be older. The carol was once part of a much longer ballad that today survives only in a pair of black letter broadsides. This is a Cornish version, from William Sandys' Christmas Carols Ancient and Modern, published in 1833.

Watch for lever changes in measures 4 and 8.

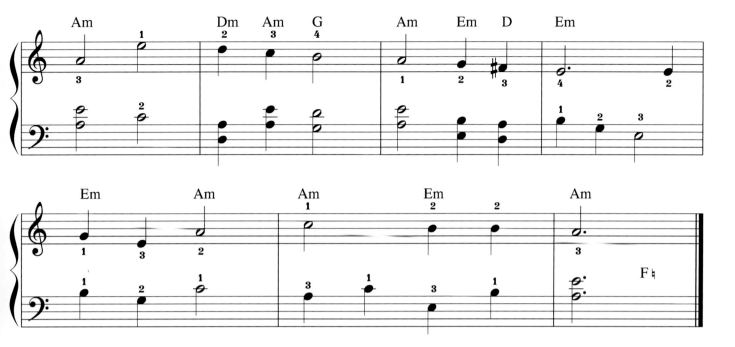

Let all that are to mirth inclined,
Consider well and bear in mind,
What our God for us has done
In sending his beloved Son.

The twenty-fifth day of December
We have good cause to remember:
In Bethlehem, upon that morn,
There was a blessed Messiah born.

But mark how all things came to pass
The inn and lodging fillèd was,
That they could find no room at all
But in a lowly oxen stall.

Near Bethlehem some shepherds keep
Their flock and herd of feeding sheep,
To whom God's angels did appear,
Which put the shepherds in great fear.

"Prepare and go," the angel said,
"To Bethlehem, be not afraid:
There you shall find, this blessèd morn,
The princely Babe, sweet Jesus, born."

With thankful heart, and joyful mind,
The shepherds went, this babe to find;
And as the heavenly angel told,
They did our Saviour, Christ, behold.

Three eastern wise men from afar,
Directed by a glorious star,
Came boldly on, and made no stay
Until they came where Jesus lay.

And being come unto that place
Where the blessed Messiah was,
They humbly laid before his feet
Their gifts of gold and incense sweet.

See how the Lord of heaven and earth
Shewd himself lowly in his birth;
A sweet example of mankind
To learn to bear an humble mind.

No costly robes, nor rich attire,
Did Jesus Christ our Lord desire;
Nor music, nor sweet harmony,
Till glorious angels from on high

Did in melodious manner sing,
Praises unto our Heavenly King:
"All honour, glory, might and power,
Be unto Christ, our Saviour!"

Let all your songs and praises be
Unto his heavenly majesty,
And evermore amongst our mirth
Remember Christ our Saviour's birth.

Lo, How a Rose

Es ist ein' Ros' Entsprungen

With its beautiful medieval imagery of the rose amidst the snow, this is one of the best known and most loved carols. The carol is believed to have originated in the cathedral city of Trier, in the fifteenth century. There is a famous seventeenth century setting by Praetorius. The well known English text was written in the late nineteenth century by Theodore Baker and Harriet R. Spaeth.

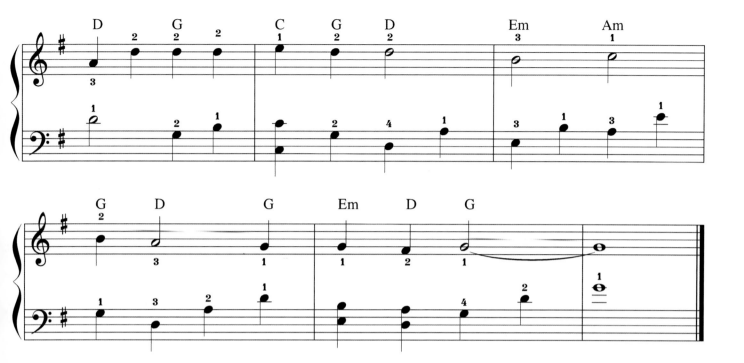

Lo, how a Rose e'er blooming
From tender stem hath sprung!
Of Jesse's lineage coming,
As those of old have sung.
It came, a flower bright,
Amid the cold of winter,
When half spent was the night.

Isaiah hath foretold it
In words of promise sure,
And Mary's arms enfold it,
A virgin meek and pure.
Through God's eternal will
This Child to her is given
At midnight calm and still.

This Flower, whose fragrance tender,
With sweetness fills the air,
Dispels with glorious splendor
The darkness everywhere;
True Man, yet very God,
From sin and death He saves us,
And lightens every load.

Es ist ein Ros' entsprungen
Aus einer Wurzel zart.
Wie uns die Alten sungen,
Aus Jesse kam die Art
Und hat ein Blümlein bracht,
Mitten im kalten Winter,
Wohl zu der halben Nacht.

Das Röslein das ich meine,
Darvon Esaias sagt:
Hat uns gebracht alleine
Marie, die reine Magd.
Aus Gottes ew'gem Rhat
Hat sie ein Kind geboren,
Wohl zu der halben Nacht.

Das Blümelein so kleine,
Das duftet uns so süß,
Mit seinem hellen Scheine
Vertreibt's die Finsternis.
Wahr' Mensch und wahrer Gott,
Hilft uns aus allem Leide,
Rettet von Sünd' und Tod.

March des Rois
March of the Kings

A Provençal carol written to accompany the traditional pageant of the three kings, which traveled through Provence at Epiphany. These processions, sometimes complete with camels, made their way through the villages and towns, stopping at churches to present the gifts of the kings to the crèche. The pageant itself dates to medieval times. The carol is from the eighteenth century. The tune began life as a military march in the seventeenth century, and is sometimes attributed to Lully. Bizet used the melody to evoke the Provençal countryside in his music for Daudet's drama, L'Arlésienne.

Sharp the G above middle C.

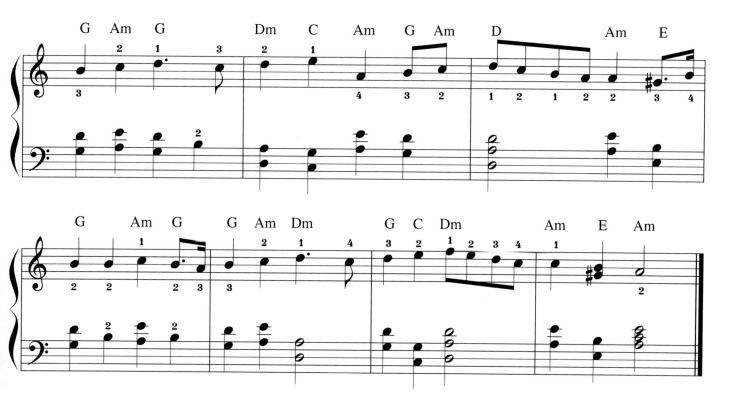

Ce matin j'ai rencontré le train
De trois grands Rois qui allaient en voyage,
De bon matin j'ai rencontré le train
De trois grands Rois dessus le grand chemin.
Venaient d'abord des gardes du corps,
Des gens armés avec trente petits pages,
Venaient d'abord des gardes du corps
Des gens armés dessus leurs just'au corps.

Puis sur un char, parmi les étendards
Venaient trois rois modestes comme d'anges,
Puis sur un char, parmi les étendards,
C'est Melchior, Balthazar et Gaspard.
L'étoile luit qui les Rois conduit
Par longs chemins devant une pauvre étable,
L'étoile luit qui les Rois conduit
Par longs chemins devant l'humble réduit.

Au fils de Dieu qui est né en ces lieux
Ils viennent tous présenter leurs hommages,
Au fils de Dieu qui est né en ces lieux
Ils viennent tous présenter leurs doux voeux.
Or, myrrhe, encens sont les beaux présents
Qu'ils ont porté à cet Enfant adorable
Or, myrrhe, encens sont les beaux présents
Qu'ils ont porté à ce divin Enfant.

On this day I met upon the road
Three great kings, who had traveled from afar.
On this day I met upon the road
Three great kings who followed a bright star.
First came the guards dressed in golden livery,
Guarding a gift from a royal treasury.
Then came young pages and minstrels fair,
Lifting voices in hymns so rare.

Last came the kings, amongst the banners bright.
Three great kings, like angels in their might.
There came the kings, following the star,
Melchior, Gaspard and Balthazar.
The shining star before them led.
By long roads, to a humble oxen shed.
Three great kings, who had traveled far,
Were led to a stable by the guiding star.

In that place lay a Child in the straw,
And these three kings bowed before him with awe
In that place born was God's own Son
And gifts they brought Him, every one.
Gold, and myrrh, and incense sweet,
To lay before the newborn infant's feet.
Treasures they brought from far off lands,
To place into His tiny hands.

Maria Durch ein'n Dornwald Ging

Maria Wanders Through the Thorns

Like "Cold December's Winds," and "Lo How a Rose," this German folk carol contains the medieval symbolism of the winter rose. In this case, the thorn wood symbolizes the fallen world and the rose, the promise of redemption. The carol is believed to date from the fifteenth century. The unusual melody is missing the seventh degree of the scale— an indication of its antiquity. The refrain, "Kyrie Eleison," is Greek for "Lord have mercy."

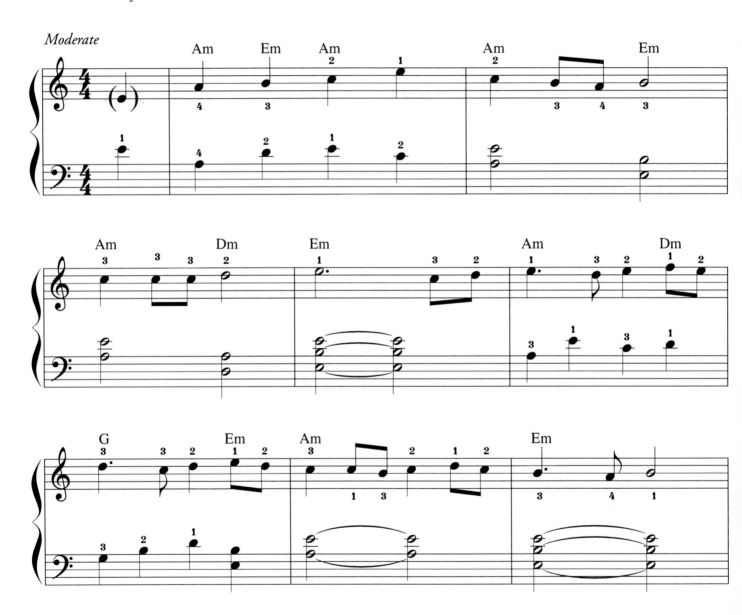

30

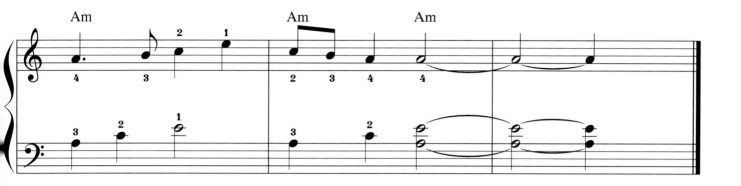

Maria durch ein'n Dornwald ging,
Kyrieleison!
Maria durch ein'n Dornwald ging,
Der hat in sieb'n Jahr kein Laub getragen.
Jesus und Maria.

Was trug Maria unter ihrem Herzen?
Kyrieleison!
Ein kleines Kindlein ohne Schmerzen,
Das trug Maria unterm Herzen!
Jesus und Maria.

Da hab'n die Dornen Rosen getragen,
Kyrieleison!
Als das Kindlein durch den Wald getragen,
Da haben die Dornen Rosen getragen!
Jesus und Maria.

Maria wanders through the thorn,
Kyrie Eleison!
Maria wanders through the thorn,
That seven years no leaf has borne.
Jesus and Maria.

What does she carry, Maria fair?
Kyrie Eleison!
A little child, she carries there,
Beneath her heart, safe from all care.
Jesus and Maria.

With child through the woods she goes,
Kyrie Eleison!
And on the thorn there blooms a rose,
The thorn once bare now bears a rose!
Jesus and Maria.

The Moon Shines Bright
The Bellman's Song

"This carol they began that hour, with a hey and a ho, and a hey noni no, how that life was but a flower." —Shakespeare

This is most likely the carol mentioned by Shakespeare, in As You Like It. *Although no complete version survives from Shakespeare's time, there are many later broadside versions. Its alternate title, "The Bellman's Song," refers to the town crier who, presumably, at one time sang this carol. Originally a carol for May Day, "The Moon Shines Bright" evolved into a Christmas carol during the nineteenth century. It is easy to imagine it sung by the street musicians of Dickens' London.*

Sharp the G above middle C.

The moon shines bright and the stars give a light,
A little before it is day;
Our Lord he looks down on us,
And bids us wake and pray.

Awake, awake, good people all,
Awake and you shall hear
How our dear Lord died on the cross,
For us he loved so dear.

O fair, O fair Jerusalem,
When shall I come to thee?
When shall my sorrows have an end,
Thy joy that I may see.

The fields were green as green could be,
When from his heavenly seat,
Our mighty Lord he watered us
With his heavenly dew so sweet.

The life of man is but a span,
And cut down in its flower.
We're here today, tomorrow gone,
The creatures of an hour.

My song is done, I must be gone,
I'll stay no longer here.
God bless you all, both great and small,
And send you a joyful New Year!

Nowel Sing We

A fifteenth century English carol that may have been written for the Lady Chapel of Worcester Cathedral. Both text and music are preserved in the Seldon manuscript, circa 1450. There is another setting in the Trinity Rolls, which date from the same period. I've included the original Middle English lyrics, together with a version translated into modern English by J.A. Fuller Maitland, in 1895. The Latin at the beginning of each verse of the Middle English version is taken from the Christmas liturgy.

Sharp the G and the F above middle C.

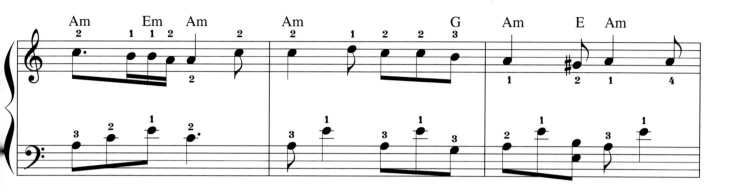

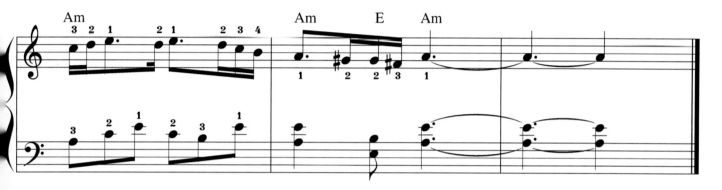

Nowel syng we bothe alle and som,
Now Rex Pacificus ys ycome.
Exortum est in love and lysse:
Now Christ has grace he gan us gysse,
And with hys body us brought to blysse,
Bothe alle and som.

Nowel syng we bothe al and som,
Now Rex Pacificus etc.
Puer natus to us was sent,
To blysse us brought, fro bale us blent,
And ellys to wo we hadde ywent,
Bothe alle and summe.

Lux fulgebit with love and lyght,
In Mary mylde his pynon pyght,
In here toke kynde with manly myght,
Bothe alle and summe.

Gloria tibi ay and blysse:
God unto his grace he us wysse,
The rent of heven that we not mysse,
Bothe alle and summe.

Rex pacificus: King of Peace.
Exortum est: This has come to pass.
Lux fulgebit: Light will shine.
Gloria tibi: Glory to thee.

Nowel sing we now all and some,
For Rex pacificus is come.
In Bethl'em in that fair city,
A child was born of a maiden free,
That shall a Lord and Prince be,
A solis ortus cardine.

Nowel sing we now all and some,
For Rex pacificus etc.
Children were slain full great plenty,
Jesu, for the love of Thee,
Wherefore their souls savèd be
Hostis Herodes impie.

As the sun shineth through the glass,
So Jesu in His mother was,
Thee to serve now grant us grace,
O lux beata Trinitas.

Now God is come to honour us
Now of Mary is born Jesus,
Make we merry among us,
Exultet coelum laudibus.

A solis ortus cardine: From the rising of the sun.
Hostis Herodes impie: Herod thou wicked foe.
O lux beata Trinitas: O blessed light of the Trinity.
Exultet coelum laudibus: Let heaven rejoice with praises

On Christmas Night

"On Christmas Night" dates to the early eighteenth century. The text was originally written in 1684, by Luke Wadding, a priest in County Wexford, Ireland. The tune is traditional. At one time this carol was popular with English street musicians and carolers.

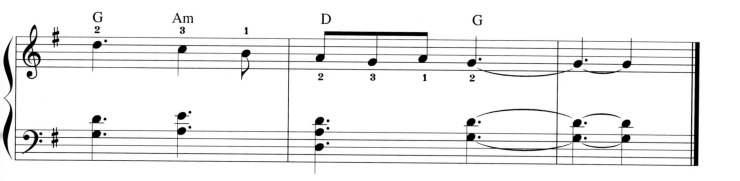

On Christmas night all Christians sing,
To hear the news the angels bring.
News of great joy, news of great mirth,
News of our merciful King's birth.

Then why should men on earth be so sad,
Since our Redeemer made us glad
When from sin he set us free,
All for to gain our liberty?

Then out of darkness we see the light
Which makes all angels to sing this night:
Glory to God and peace to men,
Both now and for ever more.

Past Midnight
The Chester Waits

The town waits were originally a town watch that patrolled the streets and called out the hours. By the sixteenth century they had evolved into civil bands of skilled musicians. At Christmas they traditionally played from door to door, a custom that continued long after their duties as watchmen ended. Each town's waits had their own distinct tune. This was the signature tune of the waits of Chester, a charming town of Roman ruins and half-timbered buildings, near the Welsh border.

Puer Nobis Nascitur
Unto Us a Son Is Born

A thirteenth century cantiones that probably originated in France, this version of "Puer Nobis" is from the 1582 manuscript, Piae Cantiones. There is also a fifteenth century version in the Trier manuscript. Jean-François Daudrieu (1682-1738) popularized the carol in the eighteenth century, with his beautiful setting for organ.

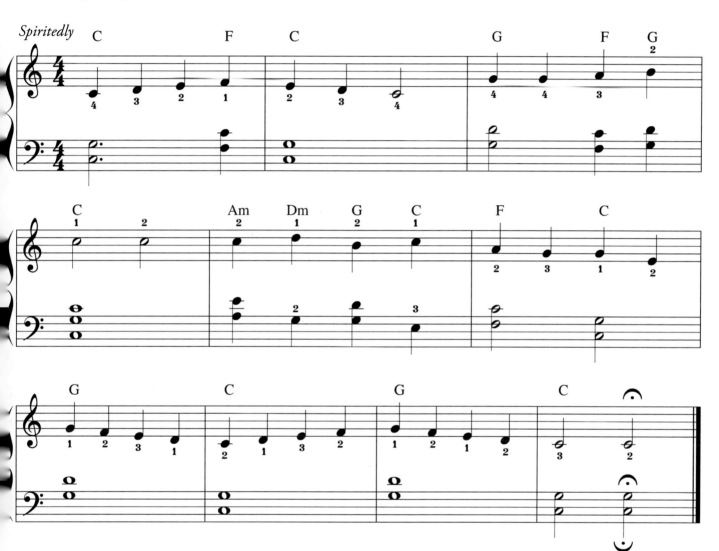

Puer nobis nascitur,
Rector angelorum;
In hoc mundo pascitur
Dominus Dominorum,
Dominus Dominorum.

Qui natus ex Maria
Die hodierna;
Duc nos, tua gratia,
Ad gaudia superna,
Ad gaudia superna.

Unto us a child is born
King of all the angels
To this world he now is come,
Of lords the Lord of all is He,
Of lords the Lord of all.

Born of Mary on this day,
By thy grace translate us;
To the realm of heaven, we pray
Where joy unending awaits us,
Where joy unending waits.

Quelle est cette Odeur Agréable?
What Is This Lovely Fragrance?

A seventeenth century French noël, thought to be originally from Lorraine. The tune became tremendously popular in England at the start of the eighteenth century. It even appeared in John Gay's famous Beggar's Opera, *in 1828, but as a drinking song, not a Christmas carol.*

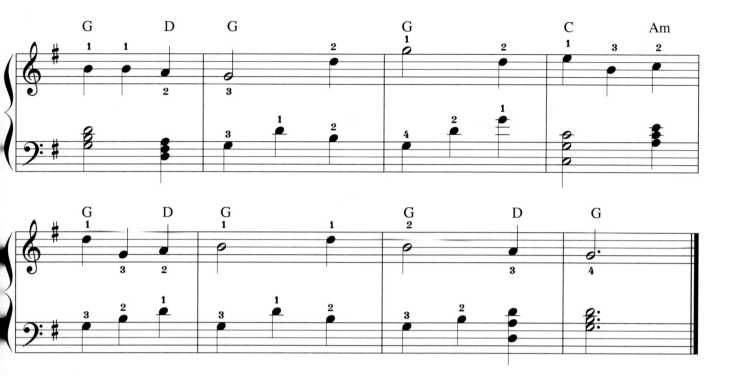

Quelle est cette odeur agréable,
Bergers, qui ravit tous nos sens?
S'exhale-t'il rien de semblable
Au milieu des fleurs du printemps?
Quelle est cette odeur agreable
Bergers, qui ravit tous nos sens?

Mais quelle éclatante lumière
Dans la nuit vient frapper nos yeux
L'astre de jour, dans sa carrière,
Fût-il jamais si radieux?
Mais quelle eclatante lumière
Dans la nuit vient frapper nos yeux.

A Bethléem, dans une crêche,
Il vient de vous naître un Sauveur
allons, que rien ne vous empêche
D'adorer votre Rédempteur
A Bethléem, dans une crêche,
Il vient de vous naître un Sauveur.

What is this lovely fragrance flowing,
Shepherds, stealing now our senses?
Never the like did come a-blowing,
From the flowers that bloom in spring.
What is this lovely fragrance flowing,
Stealing our senses away?

But what light so brilliant, breaking
In the night, before our eyes?
It is the day star's bright new waking.
But what light so brilliant, breaking
In the night, before our eyes?
It is the day star's bright new waking.

Bethlehem, there in a manger lying,
Find the Redeemer, haste away!
Run there with eager footsteps flying!
Worship the Saviour born today!
Bethlehem there in a manger lying
Find the Redeemer, haste away!

Salten y Ballen
Shepherds, Come Dancing

A delightful dance carol that is equally popular in Provence and Catalán. I have given the Provençal version, which is in the distinctive Roussillon dialect. Both versions tell of the gift of the shepherds. A true carol, meant to be sung and danced, "Salten y Ballen" probably dates to the seventeenth century.

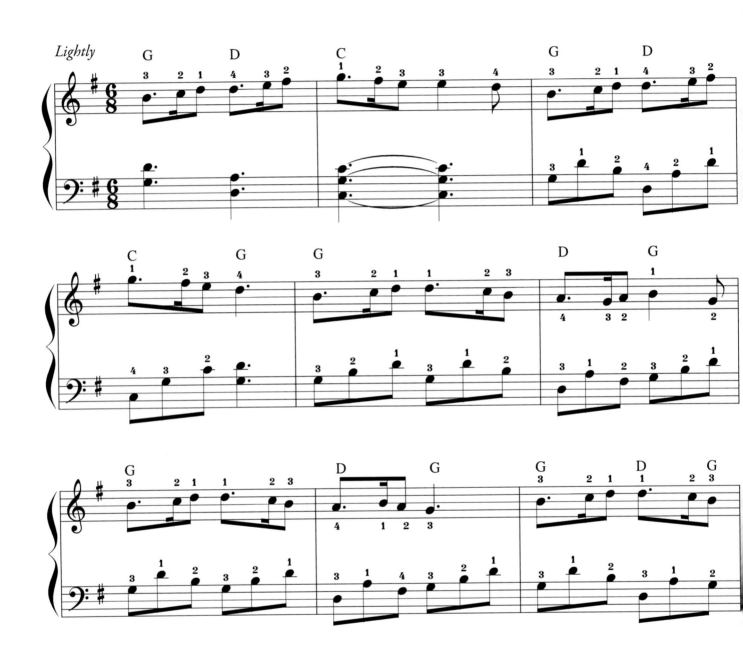

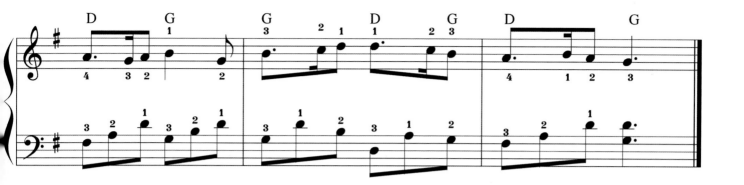

Que li darem al fillet de Maria?
Que li darem al hermos Jesuet?
Salten y ballen els pastorells dones,
Saltyn y ballen la nit de Nadal,
Salten y ballen els pastorells dones,
Saltyn y ballen la nit de Nadal.

Panses y figues y nous y olives,
Panses y figues y lo cor ben net!
Salten y ballen els pastorells dones,
Saltyn y ballen la nit de Nadal,
Salten y ballen els pastorells dones,
Saltyn y ballen la nit de Nadal.

Feuli lo llit a la Verge Marie
Feuli lo llit que la Verg'ha parit.
Salten y ballen els pastorells dones,
Saltyn y ballen la nit de Nadal,
Salten y ballen els pastorells dones,
Saltyn y ballen la nit de Nadal.

Feuli non-nou al ninet que no plori,
Feuli non-nou al ninet que no Dorm
Salten y ballen els pastorells dones,
Saltyn y ballen la nit de Nadal,
Salten y ballen els pastorells dones,
Saltyn y ballen la nit de Nadal.

What shall we bring to the son of Maria?
What shall we give to the sweet little child?
Shepherds, come dancing, come leaping and dancing,
Come leaping and dancing on this Christmas eve,
Shepherds, come dancing, come leaping and dancing,
Come leaping and dancing on this Christmas eve.

Raisins and figs, and some of our olives.
Raisins and figs, and our hearts we will give.
Shepherds, come dancing, come leaping and dancing,
Come leaping and dancing on this Christmas eve,
Shepherds, come dancing, come leaping and dancing,
Come leaping and dancing on this Christmas eve.

Make a soft bed for the Virgin Maria,
Make a soft bed for both mother and child.
Shepherds, come dancing, come leaping and dancing,
Come leaping and dancing on this Christmas eve,
Shepherds, come dancing, come leaping and dancing,
Come leaping and dancing on this Christmas eve.

Sweetly we'll sing to the child who is crying,
Sing him to sleep, little one do not cry.
Shepherds, come dancing, come leaping and dancing,
Come leaping and dancing on this Christmas eve,
Shepherds, come dancing, come leaping and dancing,
Come leaping and dancing on this Christmas eve.

Star in the East

Hail the Blest Morn

An American folk carol, preserved as a shape-note hymn in William Walker's 1835 collection, Southern Harmony. *The origins of the beautiful, modal melody are uncertain; it dates to the eighteenth century, and may be older. The first verse of the lyrics is traditional, the other verses were written by Reginald Heber (1783-1826).*

Hail the blest morn, see the great Mediator,
Down from the regions of glory descend!
Shepherds, go worship the babe in the manger,
Lo, for his guard the bright angels attend.

Brightest and best of the sons of the morning,
Dawn on our darkness and lend us Thine aid;
Star of the East, the horizon adorning,
Guide where our infant Redeemer is laid.

Cold on His cradle the dewdrops are shining;
Low lies His head with the beasts of the stall;
Angels adore Him in slumber reclining,
Maker and Monarch and Savior of all!

Say, shall we yield Him, in costly devotion,
Incense of Eden and offerings divine?
Gems of the mountain and pearls of the ocean,
Myrrh from the forest, or gold from the mine?

Vainly we offer each ample oblation,
Vainly with gifts would His favor secure;
Richer by far is the heart's adoration,
Dearer to God are the prayers of the poor.

Sweet Was the Song the Virgin Sang
The Lute Book Lullaby

A haunting and lovely carol from the sixteenth century, and one of the most beautiful of all the surviving English carols, this piece is preserved in a number of sixteenth and seventeenth century manuscripts, including William Ballet's Lute Book, c. 1590.

Sharp the G above middle C, watch for lever changes.

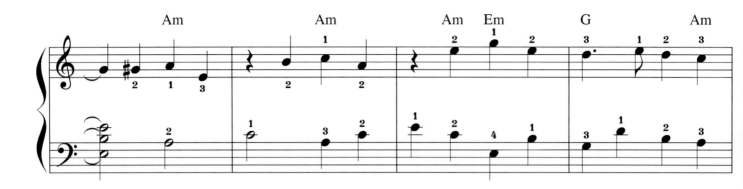

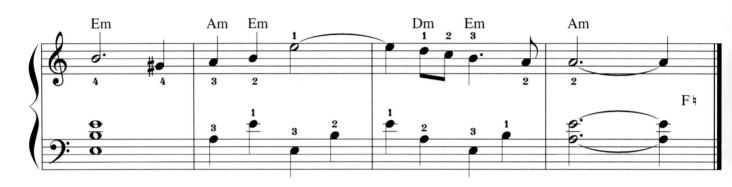

Sweet was the song the virgin sang,
When she to Bethlem Juda came,
And was delivered of her son,
Who blessed Jesus hath to Name.
Lulla lulla, lulla lullaby,
Lulla lulla, lulla lullaby.
"Sweet babe," sang she, "my son,
And God, a saviour born,
Who hath vouchsaféd from on high
To visit us that were forlorn."
La lula, la lula, la lullaby.
"Sweet babe," sang she.
And rocked him sweetly on her knee.

Te Deum Laudamus

Traditionally sung during Christmas, and always on the last day of the year, this beautiful and ancient hymn of thanksgiving is attributed to St. Nicetas, the fourth century Bishop of Remesiana (eastern Serbia). There are a tremendous number of settings. The tune given here is traditional, and dates to the eighteenth century. The complete hymn contains over twenty verses. I've included just the first verse. The English translation was written in the nineteenth century by Fr. Clarence Walworth (1820-1900).

Te deum laudamus: Te Dominum confitemur.
Te aeternum Patrem Omnis terra veneratur.

Holy God, we praise Thy Name Lord of all we bow before Thee;
All on earth Thy scepter claim, all in heaven above adore Thee.

There Was a Star in the East Land

King Herod and the Cock

This unusual carol was traditionally sung at Epiphany. It is actually a small section of a much longer ballad. The complete ballad, "The Carnel and the Crane," describes at length a conversation between a crow and a crane, the two birds discussing the birth of Christ, and the flight into Egypt. The oldest surviving version of the legend of Herod and the cock is in a Danish ballad that dates to c. 1200. In Britain, the story often appears as part of the legend of St. Stephen. "Fences" is a Middle English word for "times."

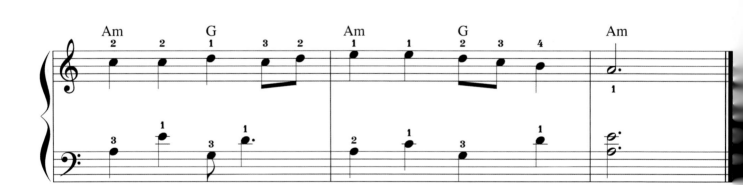

There was a star in the east land,
So bright it did appear,
Into King Herod's chamber,
And where King Herod were.

The Wise Men soon espied it,
And told the king on high:
A princely babe was born that night
No king could e'er destroy.

"If this be true," King Herod said,
"As thou tellest unto me,
This roasted cock that lies in the dish
Shall crow full fences three."

The cock soon freshly feathered was,
By the work of God's own hand,
And then three fences crowèd he
In the dish where he did stand.

The truth now I have spoken,
And the truth now I have shown;
Even the Blessed Virgin
She's now brought forth a son.

Von Himmel Hoch, O Engel Kommt!

From Heaven Above the Angel Came

A "rocking" carol that would have been sung in church on Christmas eve, to accompany the rocking of the Christ child's cradle. The earliest surviving version of this carol dates to 1588. This version is from 1623. The medieval custom of cradle rocking was widespread throughout Germany and the Low Countries. It was also traditional for children to carry a brightly decorated cradle through the streets, caroling, and bringing good luck to their neighbors.

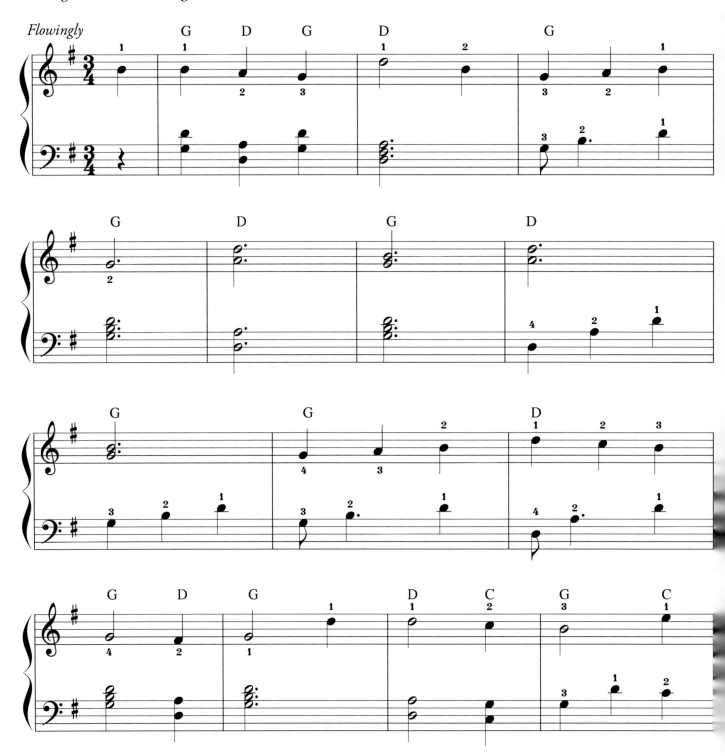

Vom Himmel hoch, O Engel, kommt!
Eia, eia, susani, susani, susani!
Kommt pfeift und trombt!
Alleluja, alleluja!
Von Jesus singt und Maria!

Kommt ohne Instrumente nit,
Bringt Lauten, Harfen, Geigen mit!

Laßt hören euer Stimmen viel,
Mit Orgel- und mit Saitenspiel!

Das Saitenspiel muß lauten süß,
Davon das Kindlein schlafen muß.

Singt Fried den Menschen weit und breit,
Gott Preis und Ehr in Ewigkeit!

From heaven on high, O angel come!
Eia, eia, susani, susani, susani!
Come with whistle and with drum,
Alleluja, alleluja!
Of Jesus sing, and Maria.

Come, bring your instruments so sweet,
With harps and lutes your Saviour greet!

O lift your voices clear and high,
With strings and organ raise the cry!

Let harp strings sound their sweet refrain,
So that the child may sleep again.

Sing peace to mankind far and wide,
And praise to God, our heav'nly guide!

Bibliography

Auserlesene Catholische Geistliche Kirchengasänge. Cologne, 1623.

Chappell, William. *National English Airs.* 2 vols. London, 1838.

——. *Popular Music in the Olden Time.* 2 vols. London: Cramer Beale & Chappell, vol. I, 1858, vol. II, 1859.

——, and Joseph W. Ebsworth, eds. *The Roxburge Ballads.* 9 vols. Hertford: The Ballad Society, 1871-1899.

Child, Francis James. *The English and Scottish Popular Ballads,* 5 vols. Boston: Houghton-Mifflin, 1882-1898 (reprinted by Dover, 1965).

Daquin, Loius-Claude, Jean-François Dandrieu, and Claude Bénigne Balbastre. *French Noëls for Organ.* New York: Dover Publications, 1997.

Davison, Archibald T., and Willi Apel. *Historical Anthology of Music.* Cambridge [Massachusetts]: Harvard University Press, 1946.

Ehret, Walter, and George K. Evans. *International Book of Christmas Carols.* New York: Walton Music, 1963.

Gilbert, Davies. *Some Ancient Christmas Carols.* London, 1922.

Hone, William. *Ancient Mysteries Described.* London, 1823.

Husk, William Henry. *Songs of the Nativity.* London, 1864.

Neale, J.M. *Hymns of the Eastern Church.* London, 1861.

Hugh Keyte, and Andrew Parrott, eds. *The New Oxford Book of Carols.* Oxford: Oxford University Press, 1998.

Lanstaff, John, and Nancy Langstaff. *The Christmas Revels Songbook.* New York: David Godine, 1985.

Percy Deamer, R. Williams, and Martin Shaw. *The Oxford Book of Carols.* Oxford: Oxford University Press, 1928.

Rimbault, Edward Francis. *A Collection of Old Christmas Carols.* London, 1861.

Sandys, William. *Christmas Carols, Ancient and Modern.* London, 1833.

Sharp, Cecil, *Cecil Sharp's Collection of English Folk Songs*, ed. Maud Karpeles. 2 vols. Oxford: Oxford University Press, 1974.

Sharp, Thomas, *The Pageant of the Shearmen and Tailors, in Coventry.* Coventry, 1817.

Theodericus Petri. *Piae Cantiones ecclesiaticae et scholasticae veterum episcoporum ad Nylanded, Griefswald. 1582.* facs. edn. ed. George Woodward. London: Plainsong and Mediaeval Music Society, 1910.

Walker, William. *The Southern Harmony.* Spartanburg [S. Carolina], 1835.

Wells, Evelyn Kendrick. *The Ballad Tree.* New York: The Ronald Press Company, 1950.

Woodward, George Ratcliffe. *Carols for Christmastide.* London, 1892.

——. *The Cowley Carol Book.* Oxford, 1902.

Index of First Lines and Titles

Other harp books by Suzanne Guldimann:

Green Grows the Holly
Medieval and Renaissance Carols

The Three Ravens
And Other Ballads

Pastime with Good Company
Elizabethan Songs and Dances

Hearts of Oak
Songs and Dances of Old England

Amid the Winter's Snow
Victorian Christmas Carols

The King's Delight
A Collection of Early Music

The Bard's Harp
Music from Shakespeare's Plays

Music for the Netherfield Ball
Songs and Dances from Jane Austen's Era

WEST OF THE MOON BOOKS
Malibu, California

Made in the USA
Middletown, DE
05 September 2024

60403924R00033